Volume 88 of the Yale Series of Younger Poets

Stone Crop

Jody Gladding

Foreword by James Dickey

Yale University Press

New Haven and London

Publication of this volume was made possible
by a grant from the Guinzburg Fund.

Designed by Sonia Scanlon.
Set in New Century Schoolbook type by
Keystone Typesetting, Inc., Orwigsburg, Pennsylvania.
Printed in the United States of America by
Thomson-Shore, Inc., Dexter, Michigan.

Library of Congress Cataloging-in-Publication Data

Gladding, Jody, 1955–
   Stone crop / Jody Gladding ; foreword by
   James Dickey.
   p. cm. — (Yale series of younger poets ; v. 88)
   ISBN 0–300–05543–9 (cloth) 0–300–05544–7 (paper)
   I. Title.   II. Series.
PS3557.L2914S86   1993   92–39605
811′.54—dc20   CIP

A catalogue record for this book is available
from the British Library.

10   9   8   7   6   5   4   3   2   1

Contents

Foreword

Though many poets write out of a sense of their bodies interpenetrating with the world, I have seen few cases in which this takes place, and in words that convince the reader it is truly going on, comparable to Jody Gladding's poems. As she herself says, her attitude is like prayer: "The whole body responsive to the world, the world experiencing itself through the body, continually maintaining that attitude and stance: *not* a little conversation between a little mind and a big one, asking for things, weighing good and evil." In all instances the connection is of course dependent on both the personality of the poet and the aspect of nature involved: Rainer Maria Rilke with flowers and leaves, D. H. Lawrence, at his most successful, with animals, Theodore Roethke with roots and stems. Gladding's is the stonecrop New England environment, *not* Robert Frost's, making for diffidence and laconic slyness, but much fuller, more mysterious, and more rewarding.

The controlling metaphor, here, is one of fecundity, wholeness, *roundness*. Many of the best poems deal with natural processes that take a long time, as with creeks changing the form of stones. Though she is well-acquainted with rough rocks, Gladding is more fulfilled—more *satisfied*—when the world, in its waters and weathers, has shaped them. For her, as for few others, stones are as full of life as berries. Refreshingly free of any and all sentimentalities, she is not afraid of hardship, and likes to ski in forests, alone or with her friend Beth, with whom she has lively conversations as they speed over snow, as they *collect*. Hers are the only poems I know that combine skiing and gossip, a more fortunate conjunction than you might guess. She does not shrink from blood, either, and is as fascinated with predation as with the process of birth.

> Until we're stopped by tufts of rodent fur,
> and here, imprinted in the snow, great wings.
> Sometimes there's a spot of blood, like a berry,
> but we see only fur and this clean, white
> intaglio for carnage.

These poems are memorable for their images of light and darkness; in other words, are good both day and night, with their poet watching and feeling alertly, always. As an ex-nightfighter, World War II vintage, I am especially astonished and delighted at the acuteness of her night vision:

> In their clarity
>
> how they seem like you
> and how they lift me out of confusion:
>
> these stars, and at the small of your back,
> a smaller constellation;
>
> this feather, the curve of the word
> itself, the riffling arc of it;
>
> a drink of water, surprising gift,
> sweet, like the simplest *yes;*
>
> also, water, where it flows
> equidistant from its banks, is slowed
> by no roots, leaves everything.

Civilization—particularly its destructions and detritus—is not slighted, but comes through transformed. For example, the "shambles of the gods," a salvage yard where "the smell of hot chrome rises," brings also the *names* of junked automobiles, which

        recall great chiefs
and tribes and the empowering animals.

Thunderbird, Winnebago, Mustang, Pontiac—
you must say these names out loud. You must
strip the radios in which the myths survive.
Repeat: *Wi-yuh returns to abolish the custom of killing
the beasts for their names*. Leave the road maps
on the dashboards. Learn the song of spawning fish.

Yes, we know them well enough, living as we do sur-
rounded by named machines, moving or still, active or
junked, and we never before knew their full meaning,
their implications, their irony.

Gladding is not oblivious to some of the most sordid
and saddening facts of contemporary life: slums; drugs.
About these she is very graphic, though to me she does
not seem horrified *enough* at the gruesome artificiality
of, say, the inner city, the collapsed vein the needle can-
not find. One wishes that her instincts, attuned so finely
to ferns and eggshells, had expressed more outrage over
such *physical* self-betrayal, for she has wit and compas-
sion, and is capable of indignation. On the other side, it
could as easily be argued that her adaptability is a favor-
able sign, and that she is, in Henry James's words, "One
on whom nothing is lost": that she has, and to a very high
degree, "accessibility to experience"—*all* experience.

Yet it is good, still, to return from the city to Gladding's
penchant for blending domesticity and wilderness; that
is right for her. She is just as interesting inside as out,
and her evocation of household materials—especially
yarn!—makes one wish to be anywhere she has been, in
any room where she is.

Skiing, swimming, hiking, collecting, bringing items
found in the woods and creeks and making them part of
her living-space are all functions of Jody Gladding's in-

terpenetration with the world, fascinating, rare, and desirable. She can go deep, and with a naturalness that requires no effort. She is after basics, underlyings, for she knows that not only beneath the jutting or smooth stonecrop but under even the lightest things, the feathers and ferns, the wild eggshells—some of them come to rest between houseplants on her windowsill—is a more profound reality, immovable and living. I hope Jody Gladding will understand when I quote another poet, William Gibson, on a situation into which she herself can take us as few others do: an advantageous encounter, for from it one comes back renewed, after

> you, I and all
> Go down to the bedrock.

James Dickey

Acknowledgments

Acknowledgment is made to the following journals for poems that originally appeared in them:

Agni: "Silver Queen," "Blue Willow," "Indian Paint"
Brown Classical Journal: "Touch"
Green Mountains Review: "But What about the Stepsisters," "The Fisherman's Wife," "Midwifery"
Poetry Northwest: "The Eight Difficult Situations," "Gifts," "Spell for Not Entering into the Shambles of the Gods," "Here, a shark's eye," "Footwork," "Undercurrent"
West Branch: "Deer Crossings," "Taughannock Falls"
Yarrow: "In their clarity"

My thanks to the Vermont Council on the Arts for financial support.

Midwifery

These stones
I unearth
squatting
in my garden
working them
into the light
their roundness
pleases me
how they look

pregnant
being no more
pregnant than I am
than my garden was
before delivering
these eggs
these old ideas
which do
come to bear

where they've been
laid
recalcitrant nest
I attend
my garden
my hands mud
drying
in the sun
their roundness.

Wings

Beth and I ski between Douglas fir,
and our talk circles around holidays,
children. Tucking them in, what stories
should we tell them? About which transcendent
visitors—angels, reindeer, an infant
announced by a star?

Until we're stopped by tufts of rodent fur,
and here, imprinted in the snow, great wings.
Sometimes there's a spot of blood, like a berry,
but we see only fur and this clean, white
intaglio for carnage.

There's less to us both this winter,
I think, as I catch Beth's profile.
What protects things by making them lovely
dissolves, revealing a framework of bone.
Though we don't speak of it. Beth is searching
for the skull. She collects them—mole,
groundhog, or mouse—and they line her
windowsill between the potted herbs.
By her sink hangs a tile, a porcelain impress
of a jay she found, and on it, she's attached
the rib cage and one blue wing.

It becomes beautiful to me, slowly,
as the angle of her jaw becomes beautiful,
and this fierce snow angel, and the astonishing
blue sky holding in its branches such birds of prey,
sleeping now, fed.

Such visitations to transport childen—
wings that drop on a tiny pulse in snow,
coming like sleep, taking you like sleep.

Sometimes I Went to a Dark Place

I liked it there
liked the way I could call into it
there is no light!

and it would echo back   light!
I liked the way it sounded, my voice calling
there is no light!   and the chorus back calling

light!   So I went often, stayed long
listening to my voice and the chorus
it called from the dark.

But once, after much calling and echoing, my voice
failed, and as it failed, the echo faded
and I said to myself there is no light.

No light I said again, and there was no echo.
No light I whispered because my voice had failed
and there was no echo.

So I turned whispering light
and I ran saying light
and I found my way out and called

light!   finding my voice again
in a chorus calling back
light from a dark place.

In their clarity

how they seem like you
and how they lift me out of confusion:

these stars, and at the small of your back,
a smaller constellation;

this feather, the curve of the word
itself, the riffling arc of it;

a drink of water, surprising gift,
sweet, like the simplest *yes;*

also, water, where it flows
equidistant from its banks, is slowed
by no roots, leaves everything.

Spell for Not Entering into
the Shambles of the Gods

The shambles of the gods stretches for miles,
a salvage yard where the smell of hot chrome rises,
where finned bodies lie beached and rusting,
and their names recall great chiefs
and tribes and the empowering animals.

Thunderbird, Winnebago, Mustang, Pontiac—
you must say these names out loud. You must
strip the radios in which the myths survive.
Repeat: *Wi-Yuh returns to abolish the custom of killing
the beasts for their names*. Leave the road maps
on the dashboards. Learn the song of spawning fish.

Taughannock Falls

I want to show you a landscape of layers—
imagine a page of your braille, imagine
the Chinese character for *dream:*
grass over *eye* over *cover* over *evening*—
you're above the falls looking down
to a stone bridge where figures in plump jackets
cluster like berries and it's colder there, already dark.

Scan the grey strata for pigeons splintering off,
slate without slate's gravity. Rise with them
to that fringe of trees, then swoop and settle
on a winking ledge where cedars, slow reptiles,
wrench themselves from rock, straining back for ground
and out for sun so that no branch isn't also root.

Look higher where a leaf, flaking off from the light,
substantial enough to be called yellow, spirals down,
out of the breathing surface, past the moment's pigeon
and cedar, past whole centuries conflated to slab,
drifts down and you, watching, imagine now,
now it must land and still it spirals and drifts and you

exhale, and still it's hovering, still airborne until
now, finally, it's floating there on the water
that collects under the falls, the water deep, blue,
and patient, waiting for the leaf it's just now
beginning to fathom to dissolve into wet stars.

for Bob Russell

Locust Shell

The locust thought
she'd die, she laughed
so hard.
She didn't
but her sides
split.
Surprised
she lay
dazed, dazzling;
she was beside
herself
or what had
up till then
given her
definition.
It doesn't mean
anything. You
can take it
lightly.

The Fisherman's Wife

So the man went away quite sorrowful to think that his wife would
want to be a king.—Brothers Grimm

You must understand how pinched she's been
this Alice
shivering in a ditch

needled by her desires
which have grown incrementally
from wistfulness, a little air moving

ripple of *wanting something else*
when the tiny invisible scales itch
when she minds the stink

and the fish eyes, glowering
at her ingratitude, and all day
imagining him out there with his lines

shining back at that generous, wifely sea.
So when he comes home empty-handed
except for a tale

they've risen to such a pitch
she has to send him back
despite his reticence

and hoping it will subside
he doesn't mention the sea change
the colors, the swells.

But don't you understand
she knows how it churns, she tosses
in her bed, outraged

by ditch, cottage, castle
dreaming she can be Pope
and no longer contained

in this brine, her blood
surges, she'll rise
one final wave of desire

to unman even the sun.

Fish Song

the heron is
my patience

my thoughtfulness
the loon

the kingfisher
my nerve

but the osprey
I am wholly

the osprey's—

Full Moon Summer Solstice

1
Near evening
the pond empties
its sounds
holding till last
the wood thrush
and the white-throated sparrow
who frees two dry notes
and leaves a third

above what
the green frog plucks
hovering there.

2
At one end of this road
the whole moon
sun at the other
makes it all light
between them
a juncture
giving rise
to Chinese characters
a character say
for heaven:
sky/hall
a corridor
lined with shadows

in which the sky
has taken over
making even my shadow
pay attention

3

letting me take on
such shapes
a dead jay's stiff wing
the flattened length of a garter snake
seared limb
ruined web
the bruised back of a salamander
until I am every tongue
this way has stilled

until I am taken up
by one great horned owl.

4

In the wake of these two lights
I wake to

no thing
that is not

wholly
how it lives

the warm egg
the slow wait of stone

those unintelligible lines
I can say now

how blood blesses the yolk
how stones die.

5

And I can say
how I will fall
away from what
breathing arc
into what
breath of calm.

The Eight Difficult Situations

According to Zen Buddhism, these are the eight situations in which
it is difficult to see the Buddha or hear the dharma.

1. The Realm of Hungry Ghosts

                                              could be anywhere,
a walkway between row houses, brick,
in the evening, when street lights
are quivering green filaments in spun
glass, and cooking smells seep through
back doors. And there the hungry ghosts,
the ones who won't stay put, languish,
indulging their nostalgia for vapors, for the boredom
of children watching reruns, for the men's faces
men carry home in their billfolds, returning
to be let in, to eat.

                    Urges so faint,
how could they nudge this ghost toward
this kitchen where I fix a savorless meal
and sit? This ghost of a boy who never
seemed that young, who, at fifteen, I fell
in love with, brushing against my screen,
eyeing my plate, this boy who died *by his own hand,*
wound tight inside the car his mother
gave him.

               But that was years ago, so what
are you doing here? I've nothing for you,
see? Even the luna moth, exquisite enough
to take your breath, when it grows wings,
gives up hunger. It costs to fly like that
at night. I know all about their reduced
mouth parts, how they lay eggs, then die.
And I wanted love to be something for us
to be *in* then, too. We were. We only used

13

our mouths for kissing, remember? For drinking
a little water. Everywhere the smell of cut grass,
we hardly slept.

But we were wrong.
If love's a lovely shape or place,
you can't stay there, not with any weight.
And if love's a way to share a meal,
you gave that up. Air, the dull vegetable
world, they were beneath you, remember
how you turned green. Look, boiled cabbage.
Where would you put it? Where?

I did not
demand. I did not look him straight
through. The hungry ghosts unnerve you
if you let them. They drive you into haze
you can't dispel, that could be clouds,
that could be anyone.

2. Hell

Ask Orpheus. He'll tell you hell is what you drag up
to the surface from below—gold, uranium, or the view
of a lovely woman stretching her arms toward you
as she is sucked back into an atmosphere of deadly justice
where they mean it when they say *don't turn around,*
where luck, weather, that breath of earth that changes leaves
and alters your course out of sheer good humor
does not blow, because the undergods are methodical
and meticulous, and if they don't tell you you'll reap just what
you sow, it's only because nothing grows in hell.

He'll take you to the Bronx, treeless, cement-lined streets
of concrete buildings, and inside one, the smell of urine, rats,
and bleach. There's no heat, only a few lit candles.
Hit me, Carlos—from the dark, a girl holds out her arm.
Carlos can't find a vein that's not collapsed, so shoots
into her hand. She hates that, how it makes her hands look,
and says it's 'cause she's cold, no veins, she's so damn
cold, and can't get warm.

He'll kick aside the empty vials of bleach Carlos provides
to offer you a seat. Make yourself comfortable—he'll play
a chord—they say if you're well organized, you can do that
anywhere, even here in hell. It's then you'll check your watch.
You'll see it's stopped. And suddenly you'll know:
it's working fine. It's then you must ask Orpheus for the song,
the one he sang to set that woman free.

3. Realm of the Blind, Deaf, and Dumb

I was still quite small the first time, and
I'd been sick. I wake, a weakened shaft of light,
to watch my father shuffle toward my bed.
He kneels to pour a taste that I don't like,
but need, into a spoon. He tries not to spill.
He can't see where I am. I raise my head,
unclench my jaw. He disappears.

The second time, I'd finished school,
was visiting at home before a trip out west.
Again I wake in darkness. My mother stands
before the mirror, her palms upturned, an opened
book that could have been a hymnal. She reads
or sings. Though her lips move, no sound, and
she can't hear me ask how can she see there
with no light. I reach up for the lamp, and then
she's gone.

The third time, ten years later, in Taiwan,
that summer I turned thirty. Unsettled
by the heat, by strangeness, by the man
I followed there who's working late, I go to bed.
He enters to undress, I think, but when
his shirt comes off, his arms begin to wave
like pennants. David? I ask. Without a word,
he slips, a gangly shadow, past the door.

Hoping that this spastic dance of his
might be a joke, I rise and look around,
behind the door, in other rooms. I'm calling
out now, wildly, distrustful. Then he appears,
stretched full length on straw mats, his earphones on.
I bend and place my hands flat on his chest.
It's warm. I sink back with relief.
But he, in turn, sits bolt upright and stares
at me, can't catch his breath, can't speak.

How cold were my hands then? How did I draw
them into waking air—the medicine, the book,
the flailing arms?

4. Into the Realm of Those with Common Sense or Eloquence

enters a cripple, braced by metal crutches
that clamp around his arms. He says
he's a collector and wants to know if
they've got a book called *U.S. Paper Money.*

They do, but he can't take it out, though
he's welcome to use it in the reference room.
Why not, he asks, I've got a card. I can read
just as good as anyone with two good eyes.
The right one's glass—he leans closer—
but you couldn't tell that, could you?

Oh, they believe him. It's just policy
with reference books because they find
that if they leave the library,
they're not returned. Well, I'd bring
it back, he says, you can trust me.
I know the price of books these days.
See, I'm a writer, too. You wouldn't
believe it looking at these stubs—he holds
up knobby fists—but I can write as good
as anyone with two good hands.

I use a typewriter, see, I can hold
pencils like this—he picks one off
the desk on his third try. I hit
the keys with the eraser ends. I keep
a box of them around because I'll wear
an end down in a day. I'm working on
a novel all about a guy like me who joins
the Air Force so he can learn to fly.
See, I believe anything you want to do
you can, if you just want to bad enough,
you know?

5. In the Realm of the Animals

the giraffe must have spoken. They're all
pressing closer to hear what she's said.
Leopards ease in, cables swaying or taut,
goldfish, toads gnarled like fists, their approach

haphazard, and otters, most earnest in play,
who the less bouyant, disheveled muskrat
tags after, snout foaming bubbles,
the antelope—listen—flying squirrels, jack rabbits,

grizzly and badger and almond-eyed cattle,
the long-tailed cuckoo, huge blue boulder
of whale. Cats, drowsy, are leaving
their sofas, and wild boar, chickens, iguana,

to hear this giraffe, who takes vistas in silence,
to hear what would drive her, mutest among them,
to try out those sounds that call up in their sounding
something *not* sound. What vision? What need?

Now will so many animals hungry for words
drive her back into silence again?

6. Heaven of Longevity

Much labored grieving,
the pine and bamboo bent over
by winds long still, and still
this *is* a heaven

of startling heights, thick roots,
and swallows—
how many darting swallows—
their wings spattered with news,

where, to wait out their undoing,
the widowed statesmen
each claim an acre,
and plant it, all thistle,

and forget the names
of their children. Such joy,
such joy, you can't conceive of.

7. Remotest Districts

1

you missed the recluse on western mountain
when you went there
weren't you home

2

transcripts that traveled light
years to reach us, only to arrive
in part—fossil, desire

3

where the ends of all my unfinished sentences
lean, stacked together like kindling, and it is
still almost

4

8. Realm of Those Born before and after the Buddha

The song breaks off—light
percussive as rain

later, stone returns
to bathe there in the dry creekbed.

Winter Walk

Toward the inarticulate source I move
past milkweed pod in snow,
abandoned house.

What's true remains there, embedded,
unstill spring, where words
accrete like ice.

If I come back with a little
speech, forgive
my happiness.

Deer Crossings

When you notice them along cornfields,
remote, but more eloquent than milkweed,
you might whisper *deer* before you drive on.

But let one about to spring over
live wire catch your dozing eye
when you're on a train and bored with cows.

Or let one cast itself
in the beam of your headlights
so close you see its ink smudge nose glisten.

Or track the buck wounded on your land
for three days. Track it and finally, shoot.
Again. Through the skull this time.
Now run your hand down the splintered forelegs.
Imagine how long they've been carrying him.

Then say these creatures
glance off your memory like small talk.
Deny they've startled you awake, stopped you short,
that the pulse you felt in the buck's shattered joint
doesn't come back to you in dreams.

Memento Mori

How lucky we are to move
among the dead. Oh,
we're in love, we've driven
all morning. Under the clothesline
I find a whalebone corset
and try it on.

It's spring, the past
unearthed again, our spirits
rising. From his heyday
the fiddler we met recalled
a name you recognized.
He's still alive? Nope, the old
man grinned, he's still dead.

We enter the ruined house.
A book lies, spine cracked,
by a caned wheelchair
in the sun parlor, all windows.
Light and dust, we must remember
how they please us, these
leafless elms holding out
their final perfect shapes.

The Old Currency—
for the paradox of its label
we salvage a cigar box.
Hyssop floods the garden.

Footwork

When Nijinsky died, they cut open his feet
to find the secret of his dance. His bones,

it turns out, were like anyone's.
With each step, our heels sink that much

deeper into earth. We have
nowhere else to go. Once my mother

crossed and recrossed an entire field
to find my sandal. Now she's gone;

she left her darning.

Here, a shark's eye,

which looks like a moon shell,
except it spirals out from a dark
center, just as grief

begins with a weight
you can't fathom, dropping,
as if into water.

What is my mother now?
Nothing. Like the news of her death
before it descends, soaring

there, weightless, true,
and not hurting anyone.
So that, looking up at a perfect

sky, my sister knew first,
the light accurate enough
she had to say, *no, not that,*

leaving us this body,
leaving us in waves, all heavier
and holding onto anything.

My father, near the center, sinks
to his knees and rises from his sorrow
with arms outstretched,

which is the length we call a fathom.
He doesn't drown, but like a shark,
he has to keep moving.

He warms his chowder and
eats it and washes the pot.
There won't be another night

like this one, he says, *no,*
not like this. His body is all verb,
to labor, to mourn.

Then hers is lowered and the earth
sealed again. What she leaves
me when I imagine her in summer

clothes, the birthmark on her shoulder
my first idea of sun, isn't loneliness,
since loneliness believes

in some other place, and I can't be
without her anywhere but here,
holding this shark's eye

in this very light, the waves,
and the gulls' torn cry

circling, irreparably free.

When I dismantle my shrine—

the white stone and the black stone
from my mother's grave,

rosehips, candle wax, black wing
of a redwing blackbird—

and toss the whole dry shell
of my grief into water,

the moon shatters.
The moon is not her face.

Touch

When an illegal radioactive waste dump caused the death of a
Columbian child who'd been playing there, villagers refused to
bury her in their cemetery, and her body was classified as
hazardous waste.

King Midas sits admiring his wealth
of burnished apples. It will be a long time
before hunger interrupts him,

a long time before he misses
the squeals of his childish daughter
who finds the dust

so lovely, so luminous, she streaks
both her arms with it. She paints her eyelids
and makes two bright antennae of her braids.

She can't wait for the dark.
How she will flit for him, lanky, radiant moth.
She doesn't wash for dinner.

And he hasn't noticed, not yet.
It will be a long time
before he comes around.

He will have to bury her in lead,
his fondest hope, this isotopic waste
over which the kingdom must rise

against him. Though he will swear
he only wanted the best
for them, for her, his golden girl,

who can barely contain herself just now—
look how she glows
anticipating his delight.

Luna Moth

no mouth
soars green
like a leaf
swept clean
from the branch
of its hunger

Pieces for Mouth Organ

There are four elements out of which the body is compacted—earth and fire and water and air.—Plato

1. Wolf's Milk

Was what my mother called
what grew where the garden turned
wild feathered at the top articulated
like tails each snapped stem held
a tiny pool which could kill you I knew
I sucked on myrtle blossoms chewed
mock orange leaves squeezed
the soft broken heads to make
milk drip out glistening
and white as teeth.

2. Silver Queen

The stuffed hedgehog whose snout melted
on the radiator wore the same overalls checked shirt
had the same bristly hair as Mr. Beavenhauer
who grew vegetables behind the stores that sprang up
long after he established his rhubarb and asparagus
with a dollar each we hunted him down among
his potatoes dusty brown shoes heels flattened no laces
once we saw him in a suit he had a gold watch
but maybe that was a dream because that old car
he idled by our kitchen Margie I've got fresh beans
and my mother wiping her hands huddling with him
over heaped boxes but maybe he *was* rich because
when we found him dwarfed by corn stalks he felt
for full ears stripped back husks to let us look
white pearls gold silk he piled my arms high
always more than we asked for he took our dollars
and gave my sister change always more
my mother said than enough.

3. Firestones

It has to come down the city says
so the stones that contain their brushfires
become the border for myrtle only a circle
of rock embedded where my parents burned
each season's debris the spined barberry the oak
leaves my mother slowly turning red under the ash
with her rake my father hurtling limbs to the flame
no more outdoor fires after that but
the singed ring remains I keep it unearthed
wondering why they aren't arrested.

4. Tinder

Tender as a gardener my father
builds his arbor of kindling on andirons
crosshatch to hold three logs he'll twist
the newspaper he writes for into cones he'll wedge
between slats before lighting their points
from back to front with one match
he'll gather us to watch the fire catch curl
and blacken the paper's edge lap at underbark
so much care for what I watch him balance
just one more log over the flames.

5. Blue Willow

A pond will deepen toward the center like a plate
we traced its shallow rim my mother steering
my inner tube past the rushes where I looked
for Moses we said it was a trip around the world
in China we wove through curtains of willow
that tickled our necks let's do that again
and we'd double back idle there lifting
our heads to the green rain
swallows met over us later I dreamed
of flying with them we had all the time
in the world we had the world
how could those trees be weeping?

6. Cut Foot

The shaded waste beside the porch we were always
shoving each other into we called the sewer
though what ran there only a tangle of ivy
and thorns to summon fear we had to turn to water
also that square pit out back its rusty hinged lid
we never knew what it was for we stuck twigs into
the oily scum we stirred it like soup we never asked
oh it was bottomless we knew it festered we couldn't
leave it alone later the water that drew us ran
between Mr. Beavenhauer's garden and the ball park
it wasn't safe for drinking rough boys
built dams there they swore once I helped
my sister limp home bleeding the creek bed
treacherous with broken glass
still we would return.

7. Close

Clinging dark starlings
seethe in the Yeagleys' sycamore
drowning out television ambulances cicadas
the ball park drowned we're submerged and
John Yeagley practices scales drunk my father
mutters through the screen such a racket my mother
insisting it isn't the heat but the humidity and we
must try to sleep now astride our porch steps she claps
her hands to release them but where does she think they can go

8. Indian Paint

It was a heart attack that knocked Bill Yeagley flat of course
he smoked but still I thought arthritis because I'd overheard
how it stiffened him so he'd start down the steps and then
be seized and turned like something blowing amazed
to arrive at the bottom on his feet after that
I watched for him I spent a lot of time
on the curb peeling bark from his sycamore
hunting soft stones at its base you could make
bright powder by scraping them on cement
he called it Indian paint he had a copper ball
to plug in and put his hands on when they hurt so
he got thinner and thinner I looked up from my stones
he took a few steps and then ascended like a leaf
I looked back my dust scattered orange and red
the trees the whole neighborhood transformed.

The End of Daylight Savings

Nick, at his usual place by the newsstand,
stamps his feet and warms his hands on coffee.
He's not wearing socks, but he looks alright—
in the morning, he often does. By afternoon,
though, he's raving, and on a Sunday, the streets
empty, you can't miss it. Either he'll curse
the boys who swerve and collide their bikes
around him, or his ghosts. The more he bellows,
the more they swarm, until someone calls the cops.
They'll find him orbiting the block, dragging
his bad leg and erupting in growls.

At the landfill, I've been watching the gulls.
How tentatively they rise, the way dreamers emerge
from sleep and try to salvage the luminous ideas
that weigh too much and fall back or fall apart
before entering the clear eye of day, these scraps
lunatics imagine true. *Lunatic,* because once
madness was said to fluctuate with the moon.

Sometimes at sunset, Nick maneuvers sideways,
propped up by parked cars and planting his feet
just so on sidewalk cracks. But the worst I've seen
him was on the Sunday after setting back the clocks.
At five, the darkness will catch you off guard.
There he was, translucent in street light, crawling
through the intersection of State and Main.
Groans leaked out of him, a dream-logged swimmer,
a man escaping fire, keeping low.

If Nick acknowledges anyone, it's the World War II
vet who pivots on his axis, extends his arms,
and sings. They converge to light the cigarettes
they find. Nick goes to him for change. But once,
looking at calendars in a store, I catch his eye,
and he hovers, crouches and peers at me,
wavering through the glass as through space.
His face is mottled, his hands clasped.

All around, newspapers blowing and gulls
folding, unfolding their wings, before I drop,
astonished, away.

Praying Mantis

Not knowing there are laws
about such things
the cat stuns the praying mantis
with a paw
may mean no harm
but even if it does
is swept up by the child who
likewise however irreverently
is only playing
and says so
as with the half obedience
one shows toward deities
no doubt powerful
but slightly outside our grasp
as we are outside theirs
he runs to the back door
still clutching the disoriented cat
at the commandment
from a voice inside the kitchen
to leave that poor thing alone
and come in here.

The screen door of heaven
closes then. The mantis remains
suppliant, graced for the moment
by the *a* in its first name.

Shoemaker and the Elves

He scores his last piece of leather.
It's late. He wonders how to keep them
out, the little ones

who leave him little
to do—buy and sell. He's mended
his children's play things.

He's rebound his dictionary.
He looks up the verb *cobble,*
then *idler.*

What's to become of him,
so rich with time
on his hands,

and so little wish to make anything
of himself, only slippers,
only wing-tipped boots.

Before dawn, he wakes. Savoring
busy dreams, he ties his apron,
unlocks his shop.

His awls hang on their hooks.
Not a heel, not a single leather
tongue's been saved for him.

What's the use? The shoemaker
hammers his workbench
with his fist.

In his window, their shoes
roost, arched, mute,
beautiful as swans.

But What about the Stepsisters

who must watch Cinderella ride away,
until the red-haired one, the one
with chopped toes, places her hand

on the older one's shoulder, so the older one,
with the bloody heel, leans out
and pulls the leaded window shut,

and glass trembling against metal
stirrups rings in their ears.
Or the sister in that story—

not the gold-braided one who falls
into a well and climbs out full
of wonder, her apron full of coins,

telling of a kingdom underground
where it can rain scalding tar or gold
and loaves cry from their ovens

and peaches beg to be picked—
not her, but the bad one who jumps
down the well after all the luck

the good sister fell into. The one
who follows, but won't stop for the bread,
is she fixed there, pitch black,

holding out her apron and crying as she burns?

Gifts

You know, Beth, how this time of year brings
with it icons, minute, bright-colored.
There's the small family huddled with a few sheep,
the kings, bearing gifts, because that's what we do
with gifts, *bear* them, as in carry, as in suffer.

This one I've been bearing since last summer,
visiting your father's grave with you still hollow
from losing him and a miscarriage, and what
do we find there? This perfect blue egg
balanced perfectly on the mounded earth
and perfectly cracked—who could contrive that
given metaphor, useless, and not to be returned?

Yesterday, after presents, David and I walked
to the meadow. In the bank beside the road,
there's a frieze I love, a series of gaps
where snow gives way to expose crumbling
brown earth, the green winter mosses, and
tucked deeper, ice, roots, quartz, and ledge.

No symbol, no story, in such generosity
of texture and light, nothing is contained
because nothing is omitted. Writing to you
now, I understand how *relief* can mean both
a way to render space and freedom from burdens.
Gifts are laid before us, Beth, we don't need
to claim them, not even the beautiful ones.

Worsted Heather

What earth is like—as round
and blue and green and flecked with red,
held in midair, turning like this
(the shuttle of my husband's hands
letting fall by lengths the yarn
I wind), and just this lonely
(a makeshift warmth, a little light)—
no other life among the cooling stars,
nothing but love unraveling it.

New Snow

The hopes I have
for this storm—
to clean the slag heaps
snow plows leave,
fill in where dogs piss,
heal the pitted yard,
as though such surfaces
need healing,
as though any sign of use
means there's been
damage.

As though recovery
does not mean
covering over again,
but returning
to some first snow,
pure reversal,
and then to what
that snow covered,
a place green and sun-warmed—
you balancing on a rock,
me wading, lifting my skirt
above the water.

But that surface breaks
through even as I recall it,
because it isn't, after all,
the first,
because there is no first—
hadn't we met
for coffee that morning,
hadn't we already known
each other for years?

So there is
no green beginning
for all the bad weather
to return us to,
scoured clean.
So after three days of fighting
we're reconciled
but not healed,
which is why,
when you come home hungry,
with snow on your collar,
you seem like a stranger.

Because this storm
finds us in a changed place,
where we must feel our way,
walking lightly,
trusting what's fallen
to recover
whatever becomes of us.

Of the Many Words for Snow,

one names such scraps
melting into the embankment
where, at night, they've pitched
their box springs, rusting paint cans,
the carcass of a deer.

Of the many words for sex,
one describes a woman
taking off her clothes
and arching back like petals
into the whole spectrum of desire.

One names a bank,
prismed in March sun,
so as to reflect the way white
contains every color—here,
where the red and yellow columbine
will blossom.

And one refers to blood,
pubic bone, and the dark hairs,
coiling—what a woman
means sometimes,
undressing.

Wild Leeks

Late afternoon, the smell of water,
woven, as the wind shifts, with the smell
of sun-warmed boards, on the porch,
a siskin, hungry or brash enough to take seeds
this close to me tying my sneakers,
cold frames mounted, first sprouts
of garlic and walking onions unmulched,
seed starts thinned, the garden mapped and
explained to you, you not listening,
nuzzling me till I move on to the next
first chore for the first warm day,
the first day swallows reappear,
flashy and reckless, I know, I know
the sun won't set on us not getting
naked, not today, and all the way
to the mailbox and back, I'm thinking that
in the woods they must be out by now,
those green flags, wide as tongues,
where balsam gives way to beech, which
we couldn't name till last spring, till
I worked one loose, one pale, netted bulb,
and held it up, and we breathed in
the belly of the hillside,
the dank, undone, melting snow.

When you reach up

inside an old pine whose
roots straddle water, to cup
the moss-crowned, infant
stone, and then, deferent,

withdraw, I know how
the long-legged spider
will cross the hollow
of my pelvis, and how
you will open your hand

to receive it. Where even
grasses can't take hold,
the succulents are nursed
by solid rock. This is
stonecrop, this, roseroot;
this is live-forever.

With Child

Little boat,
you can bear us
over the dark, over the broken water.

And so returned
to water, we can bear you up,
little boat, even as we darken, even as we break.

Undercurrent

If I whisper the names of the birds
to my daughter, who, in the course
of things, will no doubt learn to speak

them, it isn't because of Adam.
Why should she hear the names
over their songs

which she is taking in now, all ears
(though fighting sleep, her eyes keep closing).
No, it's because we've followed

an old streambed to get here.
So many currents pour into it
that, when she dreams, she will be carried

by them, among them,
mine, the human voice, full
of wood thrush white throat wax wing.